BASEBALL

BASEBALL: PITCHING

BRYANT LLOYD

The Rourke Press, Inc.
Vero Beach, Florida 32964

PHOTO CREDITS:
All photos © Lynn M. Stone except page 4 © Chris Luneski

EDITORIAL SERVICES:
Penworthy Learning Systems

Library of Congress Cataloging-in-Publication Data

Lloyd, Bryant, 1942-
   Baseball, pitching / Bryant Lloyd.
    p. cm. — (Baseball)
   Includes index
   Summary: Discusses the role of the pitcher in baseball, including such
topics as style, the pitching mound, and types of pitches.
   ISBN 1-57103-186-3
1. Pitching (Baseball)—Juvenile literature.   [1. Pitching (Baseball).
2. Baseball.]
I. Title II. Series: Lloyd, Bryant, 1942-   Baseball.
GV871.5.L56 1997
796.357'22—dc21   97–17464
                                                   CIP
                                                   AC

Printed in the USA

TABLE OF CONTENTS

THE PITCHER

The pitcher is the baseball player who throws, or pitches, the ball to a batter. How well a pitcher throws often decides who wins the game. A team's pitcher is extremely important to the team's success.

A pitcher who begins a game is the starting pitcher. If a starting pitcher does not pitch well, or gets tired, the coach **relieves** (ri LEEVZ), or replaces, that player. The second pitcher and others who may follow are **relief** (ri LEEF) pitchers.

Pitchers were not allowed to throw overhand until 1884. Softball pitchers still throw underhand.

A left-handed pitcher winds up, kicks his right leg, and begins delivery to home plate.

THE PITCHER'S MOUND

A pitcher throws slightly downhill toward the plate from a low mound of hard dirt. A major league mound is 18 feet (over 5 meters) across. It is 10 inches (25 centimeters) high at its center where the **pitching rubber** (PICH ing RUB er) is set.

A pitcher toes the pitching rubber on a Little League mound.

As this right-handed pitcher follows through with a hard-thrown pitch, his body's forward motion—momentum—carries him off the pitching rubber.

The pitching rubber is a rectangle of hard rubber, 24 inches by 6 inches (61 by 15 centimeters). It is 60 1/2 feet (18 meters) from home plate. The Little League pitching rubber is 46 feet (14 meters) from home plate.

PITCHING FROM THE MOUND

A pitcher must keep one foot on the pitching rubber when pitching, or delivering, the ball. As a pitcher prepares to throw, the motion is called a windup.

A typical windup of a right-handed pitcher begins with the pitcher's right foot against the rubber and the left foot behind it. Facing home plate, the pitcher raises the ball over the head, lifts the left leg and brings the ball back down to about the belly. Then the pitcher rears back the right arm, strides forward off the left leg, and throws.

Into his windup, a pitcher begins to rear back as he raises the ball into the gloved hand.

PITCHING STYLE

Each pitcher's windup and throwing style is different. Some pitchers use almost no windup. Most pitchers throw a baseball directly overhand. A few pitch with a sidearm or three-quarter overhand delivery.

Important for young pitchers is keeping balance on the mound. Developing a smooth, natural delivery and follow-through is important, too.

The pitcher is a fielder. After a pitch, a good pitcher gets in position to field a ball.

Although two players may hold a baseball the same way, their different pitching styles will make the ball travel with a different motion.

A right-handed pitcher's delivery brings him off the pitching rubber and leaning slightly toward first base.

PITCHES

A thrown baseball does not always fly in a straight line. Fielders want their throws to sail straight. Pitchers, however, try to make their pitches move in different directions by changing their grip on the ball.

By gripping the baseball in certain ways, pitchers can make the ball curve, dip or even wobble.

A pitch doesn't always go where a pitcher would like. This pitch hit the batter.

A curve ball, for example, thrown by a right-handed pitcher, curves away from a right-handed hitter as it nears the plate. A knuckle ball pitch takes a wobbly path.

CHANGING SPEEDS

Good pitchers keep batters guessing. Most good pitchers use the same arm speed for every pitch, but they change the speed of the ball.

The best major league fastballs travel at nearly 100 miles (161 kilometers) an hour. Curves, screwballs, knuckle balls, split-finger fastballs, sliders, and change-ups don't travel nearly as fast. Still, they are hard to hit because of their breaking movement to the side or down.

A batter who sees a mix of pitches is less likely to know what to expect.

A change-up is a pitch that is thrown at a much slower speed than the pitcher normally throws. Most batters can hit a change-up if they expect it, but the change-up is used as a surprise.

Most pitchers try to use the same pitching motion for every pitch, but they change the speed of the ball.

STRIKES

Usually a pitcher wants to throw into the **strike zone** (STRYK ZONE). The strike zone is the area over the plate and between the batter's knees and shoulders. If the batter does not swing at a pitch in the strike zone, the **umpire** (UM pyr) calls a strike. A swing and a miss also counts as a strike.

A ball hit into foul territory counts as a first or second strike, but not a third, unless the hitter is **bunting** (BUNT ing).

A perfect strike—chest high and over the plate—leaves this batter swinging and missing.

BALLS

After three strikes, a batter has struck out. On the other hand, if four balls are called by the umpire, the batter **walks** (WAWKS). The batter takes a "base on balls" and becomes a runner at first base.

A batter takes a pitch low and out of the strike zone for a ball. Control pitchers stay "ahead" of batters. That means they usually have more strikes on a batter than balls.

Good pitching form in the windup and delivery help a pitcher's control. This pitcher's follow-through leaves him facing the batter and in a good position to field any ball hit to him.

A "ball" is a pitch that is not in the strike zone and is not swung at. By having sharp control, a pitcher limits the number of batters walked.

ROAD TO THE MAJORS

Most major league pitchers began as Little League players. They also played high school baseball.

Some players became major league **prospects** (PRAHS PEKTS) in high school. Prospects have promise. They seem like they might be good enough to make the big leagues someday.

Prospects from both high school and college teams play in the minor leagues. Minor league teams are a final training ground for "the majors."

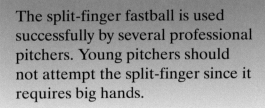

The split-finger fastball is used successfully by several professional pitchers. Young pitchers should not attempt the split-finger since it requires big hands.

Most of today's major leaguers began their baseball careers on Little League teams. Thoughts of playing on big league teams, like the White Sox on the outfield wall ad, were only dreams.

GLOSSARY

bunting (BUNT ing) — tapping a pitched ball just a few feet into fair territory

pitching rubber (PICH ing RUB er) — the rectangular block of rubber on the mound, against which a pitcher must put one foot when pitching

prospect (PRAHS PEKT) — a young baseball player who shows promise of having major league ability

relief (ri LEEF) — any pitcher who enters a baseball game to take over for, or relieve, the pitcher who started the game

relieve (ri LEEV) — to replace; to take over

strike zone (STRYK ZONE) — the area over the plate and between the batter's shoulders and knees

umpire (UM pyr) — any one of the officials on the field who makes decisions about the game, such as fair or foul, ball or strike

walk (WAWK) — a base on balls; to make four pitches called balls by the umpire to one batter

Catcher gives the pitcher a hand signal for a type of pitch and a target with his glove.

INDEX